Master Everything
The Power of Your Mind
How Our Thoughts Become Things

By David DaVinci and David Solomon Brown

@ Copyright 2022– All Rights Reserved

In no way is it legal to reproduce, duplicate, or transmit any part of this document in either electronic means or in printed format. Recording of this publication is strictly prohibited and any storage of this document is not allowed unless with written permission from the author or publisher. All rights reserved.

The Information provided herein is stated to be truthful and consistent, in that any liability, in terms of inattention or otherwise, by any usage or abuse of any policies, processes, or directions contained within is the solitary and utter responsibility of the recipient reader. Under no circumstances will any legal responsibility or blame be held against the author or publisher for any reparations, damages, or monetary loss due to the information herein, either directly or indirectly. Respective authors own all copyrights not held by the author or publisher.

Legal Notice

This book is copyright protected. This is for personal use. You cannot amend, distribute, sell, use, quote, or paraphrase any part of the content within this book, without the consent of the author or copyright owner. Legal action will be pursued, if this is breached.

Disclaimer Notice

Please note that the information contained within this document is for educational and entertainment purposes only. Every attempt has been made to provide accurate, up to date, and reliable complete information. No warranties of any kind are expressed or implied. Readers acknowledge that the author is not engaging in the rendering of legal, financial, medical, or professional advice.

By reading this document, the reader agrees that under no circumstances are we responsible for any losses, direct or indirect, which are incurred as a result of the use of information contained within the document, including, but not limited to errors, omissions, or inaccuracies

www.facebook.com/richyoungnfly

www.twitter.com/richyoung_n_fly

www.youtube.com/1stuptheplatinumog

https://www.amazon.com/author/daviddavinciaka1stup

www.soundclick.com/theplatinumog1stup

www.instagram.com/1stuptheplatinumog

Other Books by the Author

A Journey to The Great Beyond – All The Mysteries Revealed – which talks about GOD and the Universe and how it was made

As Below, So Above-The War in The Heavens- How what we do on Earth effects the Universe

The Law of 1 and a New Hope for Humanity- it explains this Universal Law

Universal Creation and The Reason for Existence – The How and Why We were Created

Breaking Karma – Reincarnation Explained – From Reincarnation to Ascension

Secrets of the Super Conscious Mind – The Key to Unlocking the GOD Mind

The KEY of David - The True DNA Code – the Secrets of our Advanced DNA, and how to Unlock these Secrets

A Spiritual Understanding – The True GOD Code Explained - A Fascinating Story about the Birth of our Universe

For Those Who Were Poor, But Dream For More, The New Guide to Maximum Self Confidence – Inner Self Confidence and Financial Success

I 1 (I Won) – The Proper Mindset for Unlimited Success

The Big Book of Universal Laws – The Natural, Spiritual, or Universal Laws

The Power of Your Thoughts – An Introduction to Human Evolution – Removing the Limits off Your Brain

The Truth about Everything – Real Spiritual Truths about GOD Human Evolution and Man

The Science of Spirituality A Study of The Universe – The Ultimate Human Evolution, Elevation, and Ascension Handbook

The Answer The Book of ELI Electric Light Intelligence – The Greatest Story Ever Told about the Origin of GOD

The Inner You – How Your Brain works with Advanced DNA

Your Higher Powers of Perception – Brain Hacks and Enhancements using Advanced NLP

Getting To Your Goals – From Scratch Wealth Attainment

Wealth, Women, and Weapons - In The L.I.F.E., Living In Financial Excellence – The Story of My Amazing Life

Understanding Your Collective Conscious – Exploring the Storehouse of Knowledge and Wisdom in Heaven- Human Evolution, Elevation, and Ascension

A Biography of the Author

Welcome to Human Evolution, Elevation, and Ascension, my name is David Solomon Brown, but I also use the pen name David DaVinci, and I am an Ascended Master Apprentice here on Earth, and I teach the Ascension Process to individuals, who may have never heard about this fascinating new element in Human Evolution, I have read over 1320 books, detailing everything from mastering Self Confidence and building Self Esteem to Advanced NLP and Hypnotherapy, and so I feel a strong desire to teach what I know to others less fortunate, these lessons will dramatically change your Life.

The Table of Contents

Chapter 1 – The Preface
Chapter 2 – Let's Explore the Mind
Chapter 3 – Erase Limiting Beliefs Using Advanced NLP
Chapter 4 – Our Conscious Mind
Chapter 5 – Our Sub Conscious Mind
Chapter 6 – Our Super Conscious Mind
Chapter 7 – How Our Thoughts Become Things
Chapter 8 – What is Advanced DNA
Chapter 9 – How Our DNA Works
Chapter 10 – The Unlocking of Advanced DNA
Chapter 11 – The School of Higher Learning
Chapter 12 – Our Advanced Abilities

Chapter 13 – So What is Master Everything
Chapter 14 – The Master Mind Concept
Chapter 15 – Mastering The Mind
Chapter 16 – Our Higher Powers of Perception
Chapter 17 – Extra Sensory Perception
Chapter 18 – Higher Sensory Perception
Chapter 19 – What is Ascension
Chapter 20 – The Ascension Process
Chapter 21 – How We Became Conscious
Chapter 22 – The Mental Ascension
Chapter 23 – Our Physical Characteristics
Chapter 24 – The Physical Ascension
Chapter 25 – Our Spiritual Nature
Chapter 26 – The Spiritual Ascension
Chapter 27 – Our Emotional Characteristics
Chapter 28 – The Emotional Ascension
Chapter 29 – What Comes After Ascension
Chapter 30 – The Summary of Master Everything
Chapter 31 – The Book Case and Bookstore

The Preface

This is my new book called "Master Everything-The Power of Your Mind, in it I will fully explain how our Thoughts become Things, I will show you how your Mind works and how you can make it even stronger than it is, I will also teach you about Advanced DNA, and how to unlock it, as I give you the story from the biblical book, so that you will know that this is true, I will also show you how to activate some of our Higher Powers and Advanced Abilities, as I teach you about ESP and HSP, our Extra and Higher Sensory Perceptions, that will give you all types of Psychic Powers, and I will do it all with no notes or preconceived ideas, How? In 2020, I learned that I had Psychic Powers, the 1st time it was an Astral Projection Dream, as I was taken to the Big Bang, and shown what really happened, this information is in my other books, I was able to learn of the Founders, for which GOD is a part of, and I was then able to fully understand the Universe, it was like I had become the Universe, so as I was sent back across the Heavens and back to Earth and my bed, I thought that this was just a crazy dream, until I go to open a book, and the 1st thing I see is a name, Infinite Intelligence, and the author was describing GOD, I knew this was no coincidence, I had found my answer, so as I learned more about the Infinite Intelligence, I started to hear an inner voice, and this inner voice was telling me to write books, even though I had never written a book in my life, I did not know at the time that this was Telepathy, the ability to communicate with thoughts when the person or entity is not in the same room, but as I laid pen to pad, the words just seemed to flow out my hands, and every word made sense, this is called Automatic Writing, the ability to translate what is called Energetic Data or Downloads that come to us thru our Kundalini or Light Cord, the Kundalini is called a Light Cord, it connects umbilically to Mother Earth and Father Son, thru an Electromagnetic Energy Field, those white Lines we see around the planet in pictures, and the Kundalini is how this information is given to us, with Telepathy and Automatic Writing, I was able to write 20 books, and as you will find out about me, all I write will be proven, for it is so far ahead of what other authors are saying, but I am not bragging, I am just stating the obvious, My High Faith in GOD is why I am able to do this, Above Level Intelligence, and the ability to translate these words into cohesive sentences, and as we go further into the book, I will be showing you how you can possess these Powers as well, many people are unaware of just what they are and how their minds works, and so they go around living an average life, and never really find the answers to their problems, but in this book, I will show you how to get these answers to your prayers, I will show you how to use your mind to bring to you what it is you desire, and I will show you how to fix your mind, and release all of the negative energy and emotions, and old memories which still cause you anxiety, these are called Limiting Beliefs, and in this book, I will show you how to get rid of them using a behavioral science called Advanced NLP or Neural Linguistic Programming, which teaches us how our brain works, why we do, what we do, it was developed by 2 scientist in California, I had to create my own version of this since my trauma was so deep and painful, and I will show a little of how it works, you have to go into your old memories, and find the painful ones and then I will show you how to release them, these Limiting Beliefs are what is holding a lot of us back from Success, so they must be let go for your brain to work at Maximum, so as we start to explore the Mind and we start to figure out how it works, these Limiting Beliefs will be the 1st thing we work on, because once they are gone, you will start to take the Limits off your Mind, and it will start to bring to you that which you want, but only if you know how to use it in the right way, which is what I am teaching here, so lets go in, and start to explore our Mind.

Lets Explore the Mind

So as we go into our Minds I will explain each part and how it works so you will know how to use it for maximum efficiency, now we have 3 parts to Mind, The Conscious, The Sub Conscious or Unconscious, and the Super Conscious Mind, and as you learn each part, you will start to see just how our Thoughts become Things, now each part has its own purpose, so as I give you these stories, I will be telling you things about yourself, that you have never heard before, but it will all be true, things like, when you were a baby, and I will show you how it all comes together, and it supports what you have already heard about such things as Reincarnation, and the Heavens, I will also tie it to the biblical book, so you can know that it is real, and some of this can be researched, but this is High Level Knowledge and Information, straight from the Source, or what we call The Infinite or Universal Intelligence, our Higher Consciousness, and the Collective Conscious of the Universe, and I was given Full Access to what is called The Storehouse of Knowledge and Wisdom, what they call the Akashic Records, for the sake of this and all of my books, so this is the real story of how our minds works and after the next part on Limiting Beliefs, we will start to explore our Mind, and what we will find will fascinate you and you will finally know that we were put here for a higher purpose, and after you read this book, you will start to know your own story, this is mine, each 1 of us has a Distinct DNA, so no 2 people are the same, not even twins, and this DNA has a purpose which I will explain later, but before we get there we must erase or release all of those Limiting Beliefs, so that is where we will start and after you read the story of Limiting Beliefs, you will know what they are, and how to just let them go on their way, for they are what is holding us back from Success, so now let get into this lesson, so we can find out the Good Stuff, that comes after we get rid of the Bad Stuff.

Erase Limiting Beliefs using Advanced NLP

So now let me introduce you to that behavioral science, I talked about earlier, it is called Advanced NLP or Neural Linguistic Programming, and it is how we communicate with our brains, it allows us to free our minds of all of that negative energy and old limited programming, as we take the limits or limiting beliefs out of our brain, it was developed by Dr. Richard Bandler, a scientist and PHD, with a friend, and it shows us how to learn more efficiently, and quicker, this in turn will allow you to really take in this material, because if you still have a restrictor or governor on your brain, this book will not be effective for you, so here is an example of how it happened in the first place, and then I will show you how to rid yourself of most if not all of these success stealing beliefs, my first book "For Those Who Were Poor, but Dream For More" shows you the full concept, so this is just a refresher course, it starts in the womb, the second mom gets pregnant, once the egg is fertilized, the sperm is embedded inside the egg, the sperm of the father will become the new baby inside the mother, as it starts to grow the first thing it receives from the mother is the first part of it's brain stem, the Sub Conscious Mind is starting to form, it has to take over once baby is free from mother, it regulates all of our automatic functions, such as breathing and heart rate, so as the baby is growing in the womb, it is taking in what is called environmental information, it is now aware of it's existence inside the mother, it is aware that it is alive, even though it is still inside the egg sac, and it kicks to show us this, every sound in the mothers environment is being taken in by the baby, this includes the mothers emotional state, is she happy?, all this information is stored in the Sub Conscious Mind, Let's hope the environment is peaceful, for most it is not, so this is the 1st PLB, now as the water breaks, and the baby is released from it's umbilical connection, it suffers what is known as the 1st trauma, going from a warm womb, to a cold hospital environment is quite shocking to a baby, this is why they sleep so peacefully, it reminds them of the womb, now as they grow up, they encounter teachers, siblings, family members, and friends, but are they supportive of child, or hard on child, most of our Persistent Limiting Beliefs are done by the people we love the most, a father being too hard on the son, a teacher talking negatively to a student, a family member treating you like an outcast, or a friend dissing you, as a child we have no way of defending ourselves, which would stop it at the door, so to say, and so whatever is said to us, if we are emotional, it will be taken into the Sub Conscious Mind, and buried in the back, where it becomes a PLB, now every time you take a test in school, do you remember that voice in the back of your mind, saying to you internally, that you are not good enough, that is the PLB, so now that we know what it is, let's talk about ridding ourselves of these success stealing thoughts, now because we are emotional creatures, we keep all of this negative energy inside us buried deep, so we need something that will identify and eliminate it, this is the reason so many have such a negative attitude, but don't know why, so we must 1st identify the PLB, by doing what I call Data Mining the Mind, it consist of looking at all of your older memories, and finding the 1's that make you emotional, once you identify it, you must first ask yourself, is it even true anymore, you aced many test, so you are not stupid, so that comment from your teacher is not true, you have to learn the lesson that memory is about, you are obviously not stupid, and so you realize that that comment no longer has any power over you, you are stronger than your thoughts, so now you have to monitor your thoughts, and look for these PLB's, and get rid of all of them, so now that we are older, we realize that most of the people we met, gave us some really bad advice, our Sub Conscious Mind has no filter to tell it whether this was good advice or not, so it takes this information in, these are called Limiting Belief, they are like the PLB's but they happen on a daily basis, every interaction with another human can be the determinor of your success, and so you must monitor what you believe, and ask yourself, this question many times, is this true or not? This then creates our Personal Belief System, This will start the process, we next have to take this thought out of our memory, and make it smaller and duller in our minds, but how do we do that, we take a picture of that memory, and we use our imagination, to make this image appear to shrink in our minds to nothingness, as it does, we notice that that memory has less power, and when we can no longer feel any emotion over this event, then we have rid ourselves of this thought, it is very simple but highly effective, this is how our brain works, we next say to ourselves, "I release the need to carry this thought or memory around with me any longer, I let it Go", and then watch as the memory fades to black, sorta, when you release the need to carry it around with you, you release yourselves from this mental prison, that you have been living in, no more emotional baggage of the type that brings pain to the body, even the most painful memories have to be let go, you can no longer carry it around or it will destroy you from the inside, and your chances for success, the more you do this Data Mining, the closer you will come to what is known as Absolute Clarity, where you have taken the film off your eyes, and the world looks so much brighter and beautiful, even if it is stormy, this is going to start to create a new more positive attitude for you, and once here, you have now taken the Limits off your Brain, so now we can proceed with filling it with some good information, so we can figure out how this Mind Works.

Our Conscious Mind

So 1st we will explore our Conscious Mind, so the Conscious Mind is our Conscious Reality, what we experience thru our 5 senses and how we view our life thru those senses, this is called our Sensory Perception, and as we go deeper in the book, you will know how to turn your Powers on, the Conscious Mind is the reasoning part of Mind, we see something happening, and then we figure out what to do next, it works by logic and reasoning, this involves using both sides of your brain, the left or logic, and the right or creative parts of mind, the example I gave is how it works, but it holds no thoughts, it just works by Seeing Something and then responding to it, so this is the Conscious part of Mind, it sees what happened, and then it relays this information, to the 2nd part of Mind Called The Sub Conscious Mind, and this is where we will start the next chapter.

The Sub Conscious Mind

Now the Sub Conscious Mind is more complex, it is where all of our memories, and information that we have learned is stored, it is just like a Computer and it's Hard Drive system, it maintains all of this information, plus it has what is called an autonomous feature, that automatically pumps blood to and from the heart, automatically regulates our breathing, we don't have to think about it, it just happens automatically or unconsciously, so this is sometimes called the Unconscious, so now we can see that this is a complex system, the Sub Conscious Mind also has another feature, and it is like a full Digital Recorder, it records our whole life from Womb to Tomb for our Judgment in Heaven, for it is the Book of Life Recorder, spoke of in the Bible, and it is made to be a repeating program, so this is how we get addictions, when we repeat an action, the Sub Conscious Mind then starts to work automatically, this is it's function to work automatically to keep us alive, so it will repeat a program, if you never tell it to stop, it will repeat that program till the end, you erase addictions by using what are called Powerful Affirmations, which when believed by the Mind, they will start to change the habit or pattern it is on, and it will start to write a new pattern, this is the part of Mind, that holds the Limiting Beliefs, it works automatically, so when we take in Limiting Beliefs, we might not know we took it in, until we find it by Data Mining the Mind, the system is designed to simply work to keep us alive, it has to be taught thru repetition the new habit, it has no filter to tell it right and wrong, and so it just records all of our conversations, and interactions with each other, it is just like a computer, that's why I say that the Sub Conscious Mind is complex, but now that we know this new information, we can start to increase our knowledge by reading books, and the Sub Conscious Mind will grow, and if we treat it like a computer and put a password protection on it, we stop the lies at the door, we ask ourselves, is this true, everybody's advice ain't good, and we can take in false beliefs, we even how to examine what pastor said to us about GOD, pastor is a human man with his own fears, so have I taken on his fears, and made them mine unconsciously, do I see GOD as vengeful, I don't for I am a spiritual man, I see GOD and us as 1, it is even Said by Jesus Christ (I and the Power are 1), the bible speaks of the Father, but where is the Mother we need both, As Above, So Below, the rules have not changed, we have both Male and Female on Earth, and the Kundalini gives us Feminine Energy from the Earth to Heal us, and Masculine energy from the Sun to fuel our brains with vital energy, so we must watch what we take in the Sub Conscious Mind, after you release those Limiting Beliefs, you can start to build a stronger, more confident you by Using Powerful

Affirmations repeatedly till they stick and become automatic, you have now just made a good habit, so now that we know how the Sub Conscious Mind works, let's go to the next part.

The Super Conscious Mind

The Super Conscious Mind is the awakening of your Higher Powers, it is the Super parts of us that brings us our dreams, it is called an MRF or Magnetic Resonance Field for it is tied to both the Energies of Earth and The Sun, remember those white lines in pictures of the Earth, so when we think thoughts, those thoughts have a vibration, and this vibration goes out of our bodies, and thru Electromagnetic Frequencies, these go out to the Universe, so our thoughts are energy, and Energy carries Power, the Super Conscious Mind is connected to our DNA, and as I explain DNA later you will see the connection, but right now I am going to tell you what it is, So the Sub Conscious Mind was the Computer, the Super Conscious Mind is the Server that it is on, the Super Conscious Mind has a powerful grouping system that files away all of our past life information, our Spiritual Information, and some really Vital Information, and it places it on our DNA, and locks it there, then when we ask for something the Super Conscious Mind searches the DNA for a time when you used what it is you are asking for, it then sends this information to the Sub Conscious Mind, where you figure out how to use this idea, or thought, or suggestion, that has come into your mind, we call our Super Conscious Mind, the GOD Mind, for it holds all of our Spiritual Lessons, and we can connect to those lesson with telepathy, it is our Field of

Dreams, and it is where we go, when we are starting to dream, those dreams then start to become reality, and what we see in the outside world, so I hope that you now know a little more about the Super Conscious, we will hear about it more in a later chapter, for now, let's talk about how our Thoughts become Things.

How our Thoughts Become Things

So now that we know something about the Mind, we can start to find out how it works in the real world, So our Super Conscious Mind is connected to this field, it is created by resonance or vibrations, and these vibrations leave our bodies as thoughts, but

Energy has Power, so our Thoughts create vibrations that extend outward, and thru the Law of Attraction, they attract to us, the people we see when we walk out the door, so we create the Reality, that we see, and how we see that Reality creates our Perception, so some of us can see things about us on a Higher Level, for we have started to develop our Psychic Powers, and with it, we awaken our 3rd Eye and this is when we get our heightened awareness or extra sensory perception, we are able to see into the past and the future, and this is how we access our DNA, it contains all of the answers we will ever need, now as we start to connect to our Super Conscious Mind, we can now just send up a thought, and it will search our past for a time when we used what we are asking for, it then relays this to us as a thought or idea, and then we start to create or make or write, and that thought has now become a thing, we do this for every thought, everything we think about, comes to our reality, this is how the Field works, it brings us our dreams, so now we can see how our Thought has just become a physical thing we can touch, in the bible, this is what the 7 Day creation story was about, how an Idea "Let There Be Light or Life" became all of what we see today, let there be Light meant that our Sun Lite, and Life was able to start, no life starts without Water and Sunlight, and we are born of water, in a water sac, mom's water broke, so we come from the ocean, but that is for another book, so as you can see from the earlier examples, how we go from idea to physical manifestation of our thoughts, we are literally turning Water to

Wine, once we learn this, we are able to then create the best reality for us and our families, the more we figure out about our Super Conscious Mind, the more powerful we will be, now that we all know that our Thoughts Become Things.

What is Advanced DNA

So let me take you back to the bible as we read the Adam and Eve Story, this is the real story, so the Atom which is what we are made of, creates EVE, which is us humans, we are Electromagnetic Vibrational Energy or EVE, remember that our Thoughts are vibrations that go outside of our bodies and can reach the furthest points of the Universe, so this is who we are, and as EVE, we saw a serpent, but this was no snake, it was our DNA, which is wrapped up around our Spinal Column like a snake or serpent, so we were given open DNA, 12 Strands of Knowledge and Information, but we then used that information, to create weapons of mass destruction, so as the story goes, GOD then Locks our DNA at 2 Strands, and this is just our Parental Data, and our DNA Markers, what the FBI uses to arrest us, so that was all, and the other 10 strands were locked, so how do we open them, this is real talk, they only open with Faith in GOD for they contain information, that put in the wrong hands, could kill us all, so since we could not use it wisely, this was the lock, now if we have Faith in GOD thru Life, our DNA will open, and we will be able to access it, it opens gradually as we age, but to fully open our DNA, we have to be responsible, there is too much Evil, let's not add to it, so this is the Story of DNA, and after they took of this knowledge of

Good and Evil, bad things started to happen, remember our Thoughts create Things, so now we can see that the story is real, the bible was trying to teach you how to use your Mind, which is the same thing, I am trying to do, if we now look at the bible as mental instructions, it all starts to make sense, so our DNA holds all of the information we received in Heaven before we came to Earth, It holds all of our Past Life Information, all of our Spiritual and Life Lessons, all of the Universal Laws we all learned in Heaven, and as we access the 9th to 12th Strand, we get even more vital information, used for good, we design free energy systems, and create things to help society along, so our DNA is our back up server system, we never lose any of our lessons we learned on the Earth, it is then written on our DNA, for future retrieval, so this should have helped explain our DNA and what it contains, the next part will start to show you how it works.

How Our DNA Works

So now that we know the biblical story behind DNA, and the reason why it is locked, we are now going to find out how it works, remember though that the Bible is talking about our Mind, so as we observe our DNA we see 12 Strands, but only 2 strands are lit, the DNA is a Double Helix design that looks like a staircase, and it has markers on it, they are A for Adenine, T for Thymine, C for Cytosine, and G for Guanine, and as they pair up, A is always with T, and C is always with G, and they run in a sequence, sometimes this sequence gets interrupted and the result is a handicap or genetic mutation, a lot of times this gets handed down from the parents, so our DNA is where most of our information and higher knowledge is kept, and as we find out what each strand does, you will finally know the secrets of Advanced DNA, it works by sending this information to the Super Conscious Mind, where it is then processed, and relayed to the Sub Conscious Mind, which is our Local Mind for use, the Super Conscious Mind is Non Local, and can communicate with others not on the planet at this time, we have to awaken our Super Conscious Mind, we do that with Faith in GOD, that is why it is called the GOD Mind, for it connects our Soul to the Heavens and the Power that made us, it is our connection to GOD, and to every other being in the Universe, for we are all interconnected, all of us as humans, so we all share 1 Universal Mind, our Universal Intelligence, and the Super Conscious Mind connects to this Intelligence thru Telepathy, and that is how we get our Energetic Downloads from Earth and the Sun and the Universe, so this is how DNA works, it holds all of our Vital Information.

The Unlocking of Advanced DNA

So I hope that this book gave you some new information on unlocking your Super Conscious Field or GOD Mind, but let me start from the top and summarize this lesson, once we release all of our Limiting Beliefs, and the Negative Energy associated with it, we get what is known as Absolute Clarity, and that is seeing Life in all of it's beauty, even when things are going wrong, we can handle it, we are strong, we release all of our fears about everything, we can handle it, we are strong, we take the limits off of our brain, it starts working correctly, we are becoming stronger, more neurons are being built and you are starting to advance mentally, this is the 1st step, next we build a bigger faith, we now know what GOD is, and why we are here, or we are going to find out soon enough, this is every humans birthright, it is written on every humans DNA, Our Spiritual Essence or Soul is the connection we feel towards Spirit or GOD, that drove us to religion in the 1st place, only now we can identify, the need for both masculine and feminine energies, the Atom, is all matter, every liquid, gas, and solid object is matter and created by the Atom and it's vibration, all the Planets and Stars except the Sun, because of the intensity with which it burns off it's nuclear fusion properties, it is plasma, all other planets have at their center an iron or magnetic core, which creates an electromagnetic field which engulfs the planet, we as humans have this same field inside of us, and it is called our Super Conscious Mind or Field, a Magnetic Resonance or Sound Wave Field, this part of our mind is considered non local, meaning that it is open to telepathic connections which enter it thru the 3rd eye or mind's eye, which operates like a mini holographic projector in our brains, which allows us to see higher dimensions and gather higher knowledge, the Sub Conscious Mind is considered to be local and is only used by the person for which it is placed in, this then connects to our Conscious Reality, our 5 senses, and this is what we see when we walk out the door, as we start to identify this Field and our 3rd eye awakens, you start to hear a voice in the back of your mind, if you have faith, this voice will guide you to heaven, if you don't your EGO will guide you to hell, this is the level of most humans, at a 2 strand DNA level, so let me explain, this is a 7 year process, at birth to age 7, and a bigger brain, an almost adult teen brain, the 1st strand, only Immediate Akashic Inheritance, or your beginning knowledge base, things automatic such as breathing and the ability to do complex things at an early age, which means you have more open DNA than others, at 14 we get our next part, but it was there all the time, and it is what the FBI use to arrest us, and what ancestry.com uses to give us our genealogy, our 2nd strand is our maternal mitochondrial, and paternal lineage data, so this is Base Level or 2 Strand DNA, at 21, we get our next dose, the 3rd Strand, and it is called our Innate or Inner Awareness, this is the point of your Spiritual Journey where you start to develop this connection to the voice inside you thru Faith, this is called our GOD Mind for this reason, if you don't have faith, you will remain at a 2 strand level until death, you may inherit some powers, but to fully open requires Faith in GOD or at least the Principles of GOD, here we learn about our bodies, we start to get fit and most marry the girl of their dreams at this time, then at 28, we get our 4th Strand and it is a combination of three parts as we mature to age 50, we get Self Balance, and it is the ability to have or achieve balance in our lives, we have kids now, and we are trying to be a good parent, at 35, we get what is known as Inner Healing, and it is the awakening of your bodily kundalini and chakral system, real crystals on the front and back of our spinal column that extend downward to the earths core, and upwards to the Sun and the Universe, this is called feminine energy or healing, and masculine energy or energetic downloads, and your body will communicate thru pain which area is blocked, they are unblocked thru love, and identifying the 7 main chakras, where is the pain, that chakra is blocked, if you have constant migraines, you are low on vital energy, and your 3rd eye is blocked, this is that pain I was talking about, this is negative emotional energy, and must be let go, all pain in the body, not caused by an accident, is emotional baggage, which cause cancers and strokes, and a feeling of Dis-Ease, at 42, we get what is called Emotional Intelligence, and it is the ability to not react to scenes in the world, that would make others uncomfortable, you are always calm, and prepared for anything, this is where men become men, and women become women, mothers and fathers are battle hardened from raising kids at this time, at 49, we get our 5th Strand, what is called our Wisdom Strand, and it is how I am writing these books with no notes or need for them, it is when we can telepathicly know that this connection to this Universal Collective Conscious, is real, and it is why most big millionaires and billionaires get rich at 50 years old, at 56 we get the 6th Strand, we get what is called Sentry Protection, and it is our protective blanket of faith, our kids have left the nest, and we are rounding out our work history, this is when we start to think about savings and retirement, so this next 1 at 63 is related to this 1, and it is Angelic

Protection, the 7th Strand, this is when most humans start to lose mental acuity, if they are not exercising the brain, by reading books, and so extra help is given for the young elderly or senior citizens, at 70, we get Our 8th Strand, we get what is called TC, or Completion of Purpose, and it is usually the last strand we humans see before death, which over millennia has significantly dropped to about 75 years old, from early human figures of 144 to 300 years, so this is all we ever get to see and that is why it is called a completion, you have lived in your purpose for many years, and GOD feels that you have completed your Spiritual Purpose, so when you get to the lower Heavens after this life, you can rest for a longer time than the people with a karmic Attachment or Obligation, before returning to Earth, at 77, we get what is called a Lack of Bias, and it is where we really get to understand GOD, we start to make friends with other races, and let go of some of the intolerance or racism, we make friends with muslim and jew, this is a lack of bias, at 84, we get our 9th Strand, what we call Ancient Remembrance, and it is where we find our Ancient Wisdom, Our

Past Life History, and Our Advanced Knowledge, all of it is located on those strands, this is why I remember the BIG BANG, I was there, not me, The Atom that made me was there cooking with all the other Atoms from the 1st explosion or Big Bang, our DNA will reveal your own story, this is mine, and it can be researched, at 91, we get what is called our Stem Cell Blueprint the 10th Strand, and it is here where we learn how to stop aging, this will show on your screen as instructions to eat better, and exercise, you say what are we doing exercise at 91, we use to live longer and that is why we get this at this time, it actually reverses your aging, we die at about 75 and this is because of all of the junk in the foods we eat, designed to get us sick, so that the pharma companies can make some money for the investors, many of which are us, but we don't receive the overhead, it goes to the bank, that holds and invests your money, the constant negativity on TV distracts us from knowledge of self, and it is done intentionally, they do not want us to have this information, but they use it everyday to manipulate markets and cheat people out of money, they have a reverse engineered DNA structure, and their faith is in the underworld, same rules, just different reasons, Do you Choose LIGHT or Darkness, GOD or Satan, Self or Others, Our Sub Conscious Mind and Recorder records all our transgressions, so there is no lying to the Council in Heaven, this is why we have Karma, and every human has to go thru the same thing, but that is for another book, at this point, you have opened or unlocked 10 strands of Advanced DNA, these next 2 are slightly different, and they may or may not open for you, 1 is built on your Faith Levels, and the other is given only to those of us who appear to GOD or ELI to be responsible enough to use it, and it contains out of this world information, so these may remain locked even after the 7 years, at this point we are at 100 or 98 and 105, at 98 years old, we get the 11th Strand, what is called the Guru Principle, we have to read books to open up this principle, it is used for higher learning and understanding, you read a book, and then your Advanced DNA, connects you to the next book on your quest automatically, it connects you to the story you are reading, and then it gives you that ability to actually use it, I say that I have a Photographic Memory, and then I read a book about photographic imagery, and as I connect to the story in this book, it starts to connect to my GOD Mind, which searches my past records for an occasion, when I may have used this power, it could have been in ancient anywhere, but it connects to that power, and now I see images on my 3rd eye, that look like photographs of memories, and things I have done, that I couldn't remember 10 minutes ago, this is how the Guru Principle works, it is The Ascended Master Teachers instructing us from Heaven, it connects to a past story in your Super Conscious Field thru the GOD Mind, and brings to your Sub Conscious Mind, an idea or suggestions to do something, or make something, or call somebody, this is the best description of how it works, how our thoughts become things, the last or 12th Strand is called the GOD Principle, and this is the only 1 I know that is only unlocked thru responsible living, as demonstrated by Christ in the bible, once this 1 is received, some of us have had some major jobs in the life before this 1, many were Kings or Generals,

Popes or Prophets, and since the beginning of time, man has gotten a fully unlocked DNA, and has destroyed himself almost every time, by using the Elements of it's Birth to make a bomb, and murder other souls, who are his brothers and sisters, fathers and mothers, war is simply killing somebody that you are related to spiritually, it is self destructive, this has been stated over and over, but it is never followed, and that is why this 1 is Locked, as we access it, we find that it has every answer to every question ever asked, and it can always be accessed, even on the go, it is like GOD is inside of Us, and it is Real, it is stated in the bible, (I and The Power are 1), this is when you gain what is called Intuitive Knowing, you have fully unlocked your Advanced DNA or Genome, and as you read more books, you gain more power, I must state this, you can even walk on water, if you train mentally to do it, this is why DNA is Locked, it could endanger a lot of people, if it is constantly used for EVIL, and this is why it is called Junk DNA, they will never open it, without faith, and they can't manipulate it, or steal it, it is a protein or nucleotide, and will dissolve upon release from the spinal area holding it, scientist can take samples, but the body must be in tact and the person alive for this type of vital informational data, remember 2 strand contains what the FBI needs for conviction, so this is how our Advanced DNA opens or unlocks as we age, and by TC or completion of purpose, we have created our own legacy or COOL for others to follow, and this is how we are to be remembered, for doing something great, or being someone great, or solving a major problem, if we work together, we can defeat anything, if we work alone with no faith, we lose it all, if we work with the Lord or GOD, we gain the knowledge of the Kingdom of Heaven, and we can Ascend and become 1 with the Stars, we can become the Light of the World, but we must use this for Good, that 12th Strand, there is no other way, The Advanced or Enlightened 1's know how to make bombs, but we write books, and only use that knowledge when needed, this is called being Responsible for Your Own Actions, that is the GOD Principle, and it is the Final Strand.

The School of Higher Learning

So now that we know what we get when we unlock our DNA, we are taught that the more books we read called Lessons in Heaven, the Higher up and the more knowledge we will receive from our DNA, it needs a stimuli point, to connect to, as it searches your past record for a time when you used what you are asking for, if you have a hidden talent, this is why, my quota was to read 1320 books in this lifetime, and I have passed that mark, and I am still learning new things about myself and the Universe, so if you really want to Advance yourself, then Higher Learning is going to get you there, and the Guru Principle and The Ascended Master Teachers will show you the way, once you learn how to telepathicly communicate, you will start to notice an increase in your Knowledge, you are now evolving to a higher being, and by using the DNA for Good, you are helping the world become more positive in the process, so this should have helped explain the concept of Higher Learning, it is how we build up our DNA even Stronger.

Our Advanced Abilities

So as we start developing these Powers, which are called our Advanced Abilities, we are starting to become stronger, our Mind is growing and creating more neural connections, and as we do this, we start to become more aware of our connection to the Universe, we are created of the Universe, the Same Light that created Us, created the Universe, so now we know that we were put here for more, the Connection to our Soul is vital, because our Soul is our Spiritual Side, it connects to the Holy Spirit, and thru that connection, we are given access to what is called a Storehouse of Knowledge and Wisdom, it is where our answers and ideas and inventions are stored, and every human has access thru faith in GOD, it is seen thru our 3rd Eye, as a place like a library, where we can go, and find out about anything, any question answered, this is how I am writing this book, it also connects us to The Collective Conscious called the Universal or Infinite Intelligence, where all the thoughts of us humans go, and we intercept telepathicly thoughts from other beings not on earth, some call it channeling, so this is the start of your Advanced Abilities, and as you read more books, more of these Higher Powers come to you, these 2 are telepathic, and it is 1 of the 1st Powers you will learn, but as you start to read, more of these powers come online, and soon you are gonna start to write them down like I do, for they are our Lessons from Heaven, and if we receive them, they will point us in the right way to see GOD, things like Automatic Writing and Remote Viewing then start to come online for you, Automatic Writing is how I write my books, no notes, and Remote Viewing, is sitting at home, but using your mind to be anywhere in the Universe that you want to be, notice I said Universe, not just our planet, every planet can be viewed in this fashion, though we may change appearance for we are then using an alien body to visit an occupied planet, so as we develop our Powers even more, we will start to receive more and that is what we will talk about next.

So What is Master Everything

So in order to Master Everything, you have to be taught the truth, and then you can become the master of your own destiny, so now we have reached a point, where you know how your mind works, and you know about DNA, but there is still more to learn about us humans, and as you gain this knowledge you will start to be the master of everything you do, every answers is already written on our Advanced DNA, and only needs Faith in GOD to use it, we read good books which connect us emotionally to the story we are reading or listening to, so we start to take this into our Sub Conscious Mind, and it is stored in our memories, and it becomes part of you as a result, and it happens automatically or unconsciously, so you gain a new power, and as you learn to use that power, you then become the Master of that Power, and that is how you build up your abilities, we all take in information this way, and it is why our lives are how they are, so the more we learn, the Stronger we become as we start to evolve into a higher being on Earth, and we still have more to go as I take you on a journey, where we learn to use our Creative Imagination, to get us some answers from our friends, this is Mental Work.

The Master Mind Concept

In the Early 1900's, Napoleon Hill came up with a concept, called the Master Mind Concept, he had written a book called Think and Grow Rich, and it contained a formula to help you figure out thru examples of Rich Men, how they became successful, so what we would do if no one was around, was to put Influential People in our lives into the roles of your business team, and as you walked around the room, you would use your imagination to think about what they would think about your question, and the Answers they would give you, and as you did this the answers would start to help you figure out your problem, you were getting a different perspective on your problem, and now it is solved, I bring this up, so that you will start to build up your Creative Imagination and your 3rd Eye, 1st there is Creative Imagination, where you see images on your 3rd Eye screen above the eyes at the forehead, or Creative Expression, where you hear voices in the back of your mind that are helpful and warm, this is our inner self communicating with us once found, so imagination is the key to mastering everything, because as we build our imagination up, our inner vision gets clearer, we are using repetition to imprint it on the Sub Conscious Mind, then it will become automatic, that is what the Sub Conscious does it makes it automatic, now that we have have figured out how to create thru our

Creative Imagination, we are finally ready to master our own minds.

Mastering the Mind

So now we know that the Super Conscious connects us to the information, and the Sub Conscious when told repeatedly will eventually start doing it automatically, we now have a way to get all of the information, and allow the Sub Conscious Mind to get even stronger, as we connect to more books, we get more ideas and different perspectives, which then shapes our Understanding, and we get bigger ideas as a result, when we apply Higher Learning to the Equation, we start to really see our intelligence, I am not a college graduate, however I probably know more about the Universe than 99% of the Population, this is a result of this Higher Learning, the more Advanced Abilities we build, the stronger our mind will become, and we will start to understand that this was GOD's Gift to us humans, DNA which held the answers, and led to us discovering our Spiritual Selves, our Soul was starting to Evolve, and we were becoming greater, so as we gain greater control of our own minds, and we start to learn about more of our powers, we are finally starting to master our minds.

Our Higher Powers of Perception

I already told you how we can see our past lives, once we open our DNA to Past Life

Rememberance, but what if I told you that we could see into the future, and change it, would you believe me, well we can and it is called Foresight, the ability to see into the Future, and I will explain how it works, these are called our Higher Powers of Perception, and can be learned, so I will start this lesson with a story about Chess, I had a millionaire friend I was living with, and he would teach me certain things, as I listened to him, one day he asked me if I knew how to play chess, I didn't, so he said let me teach you, the 1st thing he explained were the Pieces, how you could substitute your pieces for family and friends, and see how it plays out, what is important to you and why, this was just getting me interested, then he explained the Rules of the Game, Move your pieces strategically to capture the other players King, Check Mate, but each piece has a different movement, so you have to be strategic, so he was teaching me strategy, next he said the way to win this game is to be able to think 3 to 5 moves ahead, so as I heard this, something clicked in my head, I said if I can apply that to everything I do, thinking 5, 10, 20 moves ahead, I could avoid a lot of problems in my life, so this was the development of what is called Foresight, it is the ability to see into the future, as you start to see everything you do in this way, you are then able to avoid any problems, because you have already thought of the problem, and a solution, some call this precognition, and it is what we call our Higher Powers of Perception, as we look at the ESP and HSP parts of this book, we will start to gain many powers, and if we learn to use them correctly, we can do great things, so this is just 1 of the Powers, other forms of this perception, include multi tasking, visualization, problem solving and decision making, and as you start to integrate these powers into your life, you will start to see life as so much easier, because you are already aware of what can happen at any time, and you have prepared properly for it, so I hope that this part gave you some insight into our Higher Powers of Perception, Foresight is considered a Psychic Power, and as you build up the ability, it will continue to grow, as it becomes automatic to your Sub Conscious Mind, so the next 2 parts are going to talk about our Extra and Higher Sensory Perceptions, what they are and how do we develop them, so let's continue.

Extra Sensory Perception

So we grew up knowing we had 5 senses, hearing, seeing tasting, touching and smelling, but here we are going to learn about our 6th

Sense, our Psychic Abilities, these open up at the 6th Chakra or our 3rd Eye Chakra, and they allow us to do some incredible things, you already heard about how I use Telepathy to write my books, with Telepathy, we can transmit and receive signals or impressions, thru our 3rd Eye from beings and entities that are not on Earth at this time, this is done thru our Super Conscious Field which opens and accesses our DNA, and allows us to reach the Super Conscious Level that connects us to our Higher States of Consciousness, and I already talked about our 9th Strand of DNA called our Past Life Rememberance, it is also called Retro Cognition, and it is the ability to perceive the past, so we can see where we may have encountered trouble in a past life, this way, we don't have to repeat it, we also get Psychometry, which is the ability to obtain information thru touch, we just touch somebody, and our 3rd Eye goes into overdrive, and we are then able to read their minds, or tell them about some obstruction or disease in the body, we also get something called Dermo Optical Perception, which is the ability of a person to see inside their own bodies, it is like what superman does with his x ray vision, we also get what is called Dream Telepathy, where we are able to obtain and send information thru our dreams to others, many have heard of Dowsing, the ability to detect water under the ground, using a Dowsing Rod, and we also get what is called our Clair's, there is Clairvoyance, which is the ability to see things happen from far away, Clairaudient, the ability to hear voices from a distance, and Clairsentience, which is the ability to see and read peoples emotional state, once we have developed these Powers, they start to activate what is called our Intuition, or what is called Intuitive knowing, so we are given the Powers to perceive all of these phenomenas, and they are real, most people never develop their Extra Sensory Perception, because they are told that it isn't real, and even though they may have experienced something to make them think they are Psychic, they start to doubt their Powers, and so their Powers lay dormant inside of them, never to be used to help man make life better, GOD has given us these Gifts, and we can learn how to use them to make our life that much easier, so these are your 6th Sense, and the beginning of your Psychic Abilities, but it gets better, so let's go to the next part, and talk about our Higher Sensory Perception.

Higher Sensory Perception

So now we are going to talk about our Higher Sensory Perception, or our 7th Sense, and these open up after we open our Advanced DNA and open the 12th Strand, called the GOD principle, we are becoming like them Super heroes of Marvel comics, once we start activating these Higher Powers, so 1st we get Remote Viewing, which is the ability to use our minds to go anywhere in the world we want mentally, and even hear conversations, and we can even see what these places look like, even if they are not on Earth, some of us can even see the other planets, and visit them with our psychic abilities, we also get what is called Astral Projection, which is an out of body experience, where our Soul detaches from the body and can travel to those places, I talked about this earlier when I witnessed the Big Bang, we also get Automatic Writing, which is how I am writing this book, it is simply writing without Conscious Intent, this means, that I am able to write these words, and I don't even have to think about what I am writing, all of it will be correct and truthful, so this is Automatic Writing, we get what is called

Bi Location, and that is the ability to be in 2 places at once, our body is here, but our mind is in some other place, and we are able to be in both locations at the same time, we learn Energy Medicine, which is healing with Spiritual Energy, what Jesus Christ was doing in the Bible, and Psychic Surgery, which is the ability to remove disease by using Energy Techniques, we get Ergokinesis, which is the ability to influence movement with no direct contact, this is similar to Telekinesis, which is the ability to control and manipulate matter with your mind, this is how they built the pyramids, we also get Levitation which is the ability to fly or float, this 1 is spoke of in the Bible, as Jesus Christ walked on Water, the story is real, and this is 1 of the powers, we get Materialization, which is the ability to make or create matter from nothing, like Ryu Ken in Street Fighter, when he made the Fireballs, we also get channeling or mediumship, which is the ability to communicate with spirits, we also get what is called Petrification, which is the ability to turn people to Stone with our Eyes like Medusa, this should remind you of the story of lot in the bible, as his wife was turned to stone, when she looked back at Sodom and Gomorrah, we also gain the ability to make Prophecy, which is the ability to foretell events, it is what Nostradamus was using for his predictions, we also get pyrokinesis, which is the ability to control fire with our minds, this is like Firestarter the movie, we also get Shape Shifting, which is the ability to change shape into anything we want, I know this sounds incredible, but it is real, we do this all the time as some of us transmigrate to become flowers and lower animals, due to their desire to experience life as these things, we get Thoughtography, or the ability to transfer or impress images using our mind, it is what Magicians do, when they read Cards, we get Xenoglossy, which is the ability to speak and understand a foreign language, even though we have never heard it before, and we may also get visitation from the Higher ups, which we will call Witnessing, so these are our Higher Sensory Powers, they only open after we have reached and unlocked our Advanced DNA to the 12th Strand, which I talked about earlier, and once we receive these Powers, we have to be responsible for how we use them, that is why our DNA was Locked in the 1st Place, because we learned of these Powers and started to use them in the wrong way, so we must be very careful, not to let that happen again, as we go to the next part about Ascension, and the secrets to it, you will see the correlation between what we have heard in this book, and how it relates to biblical scripture, so the Ascension Process, is the Story of Jesus Christ, as he laid on the cross, and the Story behind it, Jesus Christ just had all of his DNA open and his Higher Powers were activated, that is why Jesus Christ was able to do some amazing things, and we can have those same powers, but we must use them for good, and not fall into the same trap as Adam and Eve, so now we will learn the Full Ascension Process, and that will close this book, but I want you to remember that we are Spiritual Beings in Earth Created Bodies, and what we do with our Powers can either make us or break us, so we must try to stay in the Light of GOD, and use our Powers for Good.

The Ascension Process

So now that we have learned how our Mind works, how our Thoughts become Things, and how we can make it automatic using the Sub Conscious Mind, we also learned about

Advanced DNA, how it opens or unlocks over time, in order to unlock our DNA quicker, we need to gain more spiritual awareness, we do this by reading books on spirituality, which brings us closer to GOD, the More faith we have, the more the DNA opens, and we have learned about our Higher Powers of Thought and Intelligence, the Powers of Perception, ESP, and HSP, and how we can use the 11th Strand Guru Principle and Higher Learning to activate our powers, we now know just how incredible we are, now as we learn about Ascension, it will all start to make sense, so let me start by telling you about our physical body and our Density levels, so as we travel up the 15 Dimensions, we will change form, and this change will allow us to use more of our powers, so I will explain them here, so we have 5 Density Levels, that make up our Dimensional Chart, they are the Physical Body, which we learn about at the level of 3D life, then there is the Soul Body, which we occupy in Dimensions 4 thru 6, and that is where we find our Soul, or Spiritual Part and connect to it, next we have our Over Soul Body, and as we learn about the Over Soul, in Dimensions 7 thru 9, we start to reintegrate back into our Oversoul selves, we are all 1 Soul, and as we will learn, this is the beginning of our reintegration back to source, as we go Higher, the Over Soul will lead us back to Source, next we have our Avatar Body, in Dimensions 10 thru 12, the Avatar Body is our Light Body of the Soul, that we enter after death of the individual, it is what Jesus Christ was teaching before his crucifixion, the next part is our Rishic Body, Dimensions 12 thru 15, where we fully integrate back into the Source or Power or GOD that made us, we have become 1 with GOD at this level, and we will soon leave Dimensionality, so this should have helped explain how we Ascend and become 1 with the Source that made us, so now I think it is time to fill you in on the 4 Pillars of Ascension or the Ascension Process, for it will explain the dimensions to you and what we will become when we finally reach the top of this Pillar or Column, so this part is called our Mind/Body/Spirit or Soul Complex, and it is what Jesus Christ was teaching in the Bible, because I am a scientist, I have to be neutral, and look at things from a scientific perspective, but since I am a supporter of religion, or what it was trying to do, and that was to bring people closer to GOD, and that is what I am trying to show you here, how we can build a bigger relationship to the lord, now that we know what the lord is, Pure LOVE, LIGHT, POWER, and ENERGY, and we are all a part of this Energy, we are all connected to it, and we get to decide how we will use it, so I hope that this book guides you on the right path to see GOD in Heaven, and I hope that you have a safe journey, Life is built on Universal or Unconditional Love, and it also teaches us how to treat each other since we are all brothers or sisters, whether we like it or not, this is Universal Law, Unchangeable, so as we go deeper into the book, I just want you to remember those principles of Universal Law, and as you Ascend higher up the Ladder or Pillar, you actually are becoming 1 with the Source that Created you, this is a true story about Life, as we should all try to have a blessed 1.

How We Became Conscious

Earlier, I talked about our Interconnection to every other Soul, our Over Soul, and that we all are from the same Source, so we all go back to be with that Source, but we also share what is called a Collective Mind or a Collective Conscious, this shared mind is called a Universal or Infinite Intelligence, and we all are connected to it, this is the Storehouse of Knowledge and Wisdom, it is where we get all our ideas and inventions, and also where we find our Answers to many of our questions asked in prayer, it is the creative part of mind fueled by the vital energy we get from the Sun, we call it the GOD Mind or Super Conscious Mind, for it is Super Intelligent, and it is a Non Local System, meaning that it can communicate with other forms of Consciousness thru out our Universe, it is the result of our Electromagnetic nature, and those white lines we see in pictures of the earth and it's Electromagnetic Field, this same field is inside of us, meaning that we are connected to the Earth and her Energies, but this Electromagnetic Field also extends out into the Universe, and it is how we are able to communicate with others not on the earth at this time, it is thru our extra sensory perception, that we are able to mentally pick up images and words straight from our mind, and write them down as quickly as they come thru Telepathy, real conversations when we are not even in the same room or country or planet, this Super Conscious Mind is connected to our Advanced DNA, and it is how we can Find our answers to the questions and prayers we ask of GOD, this is how we are able to go back into our past memories and past lives records for a time when we used this thing we are asking for, it then sends the thought back to your Sub Conscious Mind as an Idea, or a thought, or a suggestion, and that is how our Super Conscious Mind works, so this should have helped explain where we get our consciousness or the awareness that we are alive and able to communicate with the world around us, when we became aware of this, that is when we became Conscious.

The Mental Ascension

So as we start to talk about Ascension the next part we will encounter will be our Mental or Higher Mind part of our existence, and our level of human consciousness, which is the awareness that you are alive or conscious at this time, this is the level of communication that we will open at our 5th Chakra or Throat Chakra level, and how we can communicate telepathicly with both the Ascended Master Teachers and all of the Consciousness that exist in the Universe, so I will call these our levels, and I will write them as 1L and 2L, so these are our Levels of

Consciousness, the Mind Part or Mental part of the Mind/Body/ Spirit or Soul Complex, so 1L is our base level consciousness, and it is described as Elemental, there's Fire (Our Actions), Air (Our Thoughts), Wind (Our Emotions), Water (Our Ideas), and Earth (Our Needs), so at the base level this speaks about the Mind and how it interacts with the body, 2L is what we call our Animal and Plant Consciousness, and it is the level of all the lower animals and plant species on the planet, all living things are conscious, and they are all aware of their existence, this speaks about the planet, and how we interact with that planet we call Earth, we operate at 3L, often called 3D Life, so this is the level of our Human Consciousness, where we interact with others, thru personal and technological means, now as we mentally ascend higher up the consciousness levels, we start to operate at a higher level of being, and we start to perceive things in a different way, we start to develop our higher powers of thought and intelligence, our Mind starts to open up to new possibilities, and we start to gain more faith in GOD, as we feel this GOD inside us, we are then starting to gain what is called our Creative Abilities, Creative Expression (Thoughts), and Creative Imagination (Images), we start to either see the words on the screen in our minds or we start to hear our inner voice, and it is this voice that leads you to the next level, 4L, this is called our Planetary Consciousness, and it is the Level where all thoughts on a planetary level are stored, if the world is positive, then we would all be able to ascend to a higher dimensional level, including the Earth, but if it is negative, then we will descend downwards to an animalistic nature, and life would become unbearable at 2D, a true definition of Hell, so when we hear the planetary consciousness, we are not just hearing the voices or thoughts of other people on Earth, we are also hearing the energetic thoughts of our

Earth Mother, and Father Sun, 5L is called our Unity Consciousness, and it is the start of your ability to communicate with other beings by name thru a telepathic connection from here on earth, that reach others in the galaxies that exist around us, this is where we meet our Universal Intelligence and connect to it, if you have faith, this Power will guide you to your dreams, Our Unity Consciousness is also the start of our Collective Consciousness, and it is the thoughts of every being, from every galaxy in our entire universe, we all contribute thoughts to this Collective Conscious, because we are all interconnected to it, at 6L, we meet our Wisdom Consciousness, the Storehouse of Knowledge and Wisdom in Heaven, what some people call the Akashic Records, and here in this Storehouse is the answer to every question that you would like to know, we access this thru our Super Conscious Mind which searches our past life records for a time when we actually used what we are asking for, so the answer is already inside of you, it just needs to be brought out of you and this is how it works, it then sends the thoughts or ideas to our Sub Conscious Mind, where we figure out how to use it, or make it, or write it, we have become mini creators of our own destiny, and you can visit this place in your mind, and it is only as real as your imagination will allow, if you think this is childish and untrue, it will not work for you, it only works in faith and belief, this is not a place we can see in the physical sense, but it is available to be used by every living soul, who believes it exist, and it is talked about in song, so now we arrive at the Highest Point of Human Consciousness, 7L our GOD Consciousness, and the full opening of our GOD Mind or Super Conscious Mind, once here we are able to get the answer to every question instantly downloaded from the Universe thru what is called Energetic Downloads as it reaches us thru the Light Cord Connection called our

Kundalini, the GOD Mind comparison is necessary because once here, you are actually opening in faith your Advanced DNA, and now you are going to start to feel the answers coming from your own Mind, and they will amaze you, I write a book about something, and then my Advanced DNA 11th strand, called the Guru Principle, then tells me to open another book in my collection, I do this and that book contains the proof of what I just wrote, described in a similar, but more complicated fashion, so this is sorta like connecting the dots to your Knowledge, Wisdom, and Understanding, so this is what we mean when we say we have a Spiritual Awakening, at 7L we find Our Soul, and we connect directly to GOD or the GOD Consciousness, hence the GOD Mind name, and we start to receive more detailed and valuable information, and All of this is our Gift from the Power called GOD, so these are the levels of Mind and Human Consciousness, once you start operating at 7L, your Life will be so much easier, because you will start to build confidence in this new found ability and this new way to communicate, and the more you practice thru Universal Law called the Law of Growth, The Better you become at it.

Our Physical Characteristics

So now we get to the Body, and what we will call our Temple, for it houses all the valuables inside of you, and it is how we are able to move around and connect to our environment here on Earth, the body is complex, with what are known as our autonomous functions that are controlled by our Sub Conscious Mind, we breath automatically or unconsciously, our heart beats and distributes blood thru out our body automatically, and all of it allows us to function, the Sub Conscious Mind also records our whole Life from Womb to Tomb for it is the Book of Life Recorder, spoken of in the Bible, which will play back once we arrive in Heaven, and have our judgment before the Council, on whether we graduate to a higher dimension or have to go back to Earth to complete our Karmic Obligations, for Karma is the main reason for Reincarnation, and why we are still here on the planet, we get many chances to get it right and then we can Ascend to the Heaven in a Ball of Light like our Brother in Faith Jesus Christ, this is the real deal, spoke of in the great book, and why we are bringing this to you at this time, it is time for the Earth to ascend to a planet of less suffering so we need more people to wake up out of this slumber, and start to remember just who they are, and why they are here, and reconnect to their Spiritual Soul, so that we can really make this world a better place, so as we explore the body and you learn about Energy and how it is distributed thru the body, you will have all of the knowledge necessary to achieve this part of the ascension process, so this will be our physical ascension as we learn just how the body works and why, so now we will get to figuring out our energy centers, they are known as the Chakras, and this is that lesson.

The Physical Ascension

Now we are going to talk about Energy, and how this Energy is distributed thru the body, first I will explain our Kundalini or Light Cord, and how it works, and then I will teach you how each chakra builds you and takes you to another Dimension, and how it all relates to Human Evolution, Elevation, and Ascension, I begin by introducing you to 2 old friends, I call them The Divine Pair, because they gave us all life, Earth is called the Divine Mother for her oceans birthed us, as little 1 celled amoeba, and the influence of a comet strike, asteroid strike or planetary accident which gave us the Building Blocks for Life to appear on Earth, the ingredients inside our physical bodies do not all come from Earth, most of what we are is only found in outer space, this is why we say that we are 1 with the Universe or GOD, the Sun is called the Divine Father, for his radioactive energy provides us with warmth and sustains us, both of the Divine Pair are Living Organisms, the Earth produces Feminine Energy which helps us humans with our energetic healing of the physical body, the Sun provides us with Vital

Energy, Masculine Energy, this fuels our brain and our creative mind, the Earth and humans are connected umbilically to each other thru the Kundalini all the way down to the Earths electromagnetic core, it travels thru the body and exits at the Crown of our Head, this Light Cord then extends all the way up to the Sun, and it is how we get information from the Earth and Sun, these are called Energetic Downloads, and if you understand how energy works, you can see how this is possible, the Light Cord is not visible to most humans, and the only time, I seen 1 was in a movie, Lucy featuring Morgan Freeman and Scarlett Johansen, but it is real, so when we really start to evolve, this movie shows some of what I am talking about, but we are aware of it's existence in the physical body, so this should have helped explain the Light Cord, and its purpose in our body, the Kundalini is directly connected to the 15 chakras and as I explain the chakras, you will begin to understand the Kundalini, so the 1st chakra is called the Root Chakra, called that because it centers the body, and just like a tree, it will start to grow, it is our foundation, and it is for humans, our survival and security, how secure are we, and how do we survive, this usually activates as we become more self confident, and start to believe in ourselves, we can handle it, this is the Umbilical connection downward, the 2nd chakra is called the Sacral Plexus Chakra, and it is our emotional energy, such as Love, and sexual desire, but also the darker 1's, our animal instincts, like hate and jealousy, these are negative emotions, and the reason for most stomach problems, the chakras activate on Love and Faith, the 3rd Chakra is called the Solar Plexus Chakra, and it is here where we find our Soul, the Solar Plexus is our Power Plant of the Body, where food goes to be turned into Energy, it is a living Sun like the 1 in the heavens above, we are it's children, here we find our Identity, who we are and what we are here for, it is responsible for our will power, our intellect, our talents, everything that makes you YOU, the 4th Chakra is called the Heart Chakra, and it is here where we find the Love of God in our hearts, and our Spirituality, GOD is inside us, and the Heart Chakra connects to that God inside you, the 5th Chakra is called the Throat Chakra, and it is here where we learn to communicate with this GOD inside us, this is the start of your Creative Expression, and your Creative Imagination, you must believe to achieve Ascension, and your creativity and imagination are how we do just that, the 6th Chakra is called the 3rd Eye Chakra, and it is here where we wake up our Psychic Powers, things like Telepathy and Remote Viewing, and Astral Projection are all possible once you get here, the 7th Chakra is called the Crown Chakra and it is at the top of our heads, and this Chakra connects to what I have called the Collective

Conscious, Our Higher States of Consciousness, and the Universal Intelligence, this provides humans with many answers to their problems, this is felt as Intuition or what is called Intuitive Knowing, the 8th Chakra is called the Thymus Chakra, or our Auric Chakra, and it is like a force field around our body, we can feel it when someone get close to us, it activates our Fight or Flight System, and it is where our energetic feminine energy from Earth is stored, it controls our white blood cells, which kills disease, and is how the Earth heals us as we Love and Heal Her, this works both ways, Show Love to Mother Earth, get Love back from Mother Earth, the 9th Chakra is our Thalamus Chakra, or our Etheric Chakra, and is how we can send and receive thoughts though the Ether or Air, and it connects to our energetic masculine energy from the Sun, here is where it stores that Vital Energy, it is how we can become even more creative, and how the greatest get that way, the 3

Chakras in the head, the 3rd Eye, the Crown, and the Thalamus in the back, form a triangle in our head which is the Kundalini Light Cord Connection, our 10th chakra is called our Soul Star, and it is here where we connect to our Over Soul Selves, we have now graduated from the body and this is the start of our outer force field called our Aura or Auric Body, the Soul Star is where the rest of our Soul lies, the body of a human can not carry the full Soul, so a portion is left in Statis or Heaven, and we can learn to communicate with our Higher Soul, we call it the Transcendental Self, the 11th chakra is called our Earth Star, and it is a higher connection to the feminine energies of the Earth, we will one day become a planet, just like earth, and here is where we get that lesson, this creates a wider force field that determines whether others will approach you, it extends the force field outward about 6 to 12 feet, the 12th Chakra is called our Galactic Star or Divine Gateway, and it is once again, our Destiny to become a Galaxy, like the Milky Way, this is the training grounds for this information, this correlates to the full opening of our 12 Strand Advanced DNA, and Full Access to that Vital and Important Information, the 13th Chakra is the Universal Chakra and it connects us directly to the Universe, that we will 1 day become, we envision ourselves as a Universe, and how we would run our own, when we are Ascended to the Higher Levels or Dimensions, the 14th Chakra is called the Universal Mother, and it is where we prepare to graduate to our Sound and Vibratory abilities, this is the training Ground for the Higher Feminine Energies, as we will 1 day become 1 with the Unified Sound Field, The Yunasai that is beyond Dimensionality, and these Chakras take many years to fully open and understand, the 15th Chakra is called the Universal Father, and it is where GOD or the Yunasai said "Let There be Light", the Sun lit, and our Heavenly Power took parts of itself to create Life for all of it's children, this is the Highest Level, you will reach in about a trillion years, and you will become that which we worship, this is the Final Level of Dimensionality, and the Training Ground for the Higher Masculine Energies, once we reach the Great Beyond, that I described earlier, the only remark is we will truly know what we really are on a microscopic and macroscopic level, this should fully explain the 15 Chakras, as we learn more about ourselves, we start to be able to figure out the answers to our spirituality, the chakras distribute the energy thru the body and the Kundalini connects us to the heavens and the earth, this should explain, the stories we heard about creation, we are all little pieces of the Universe that made us, we should feel proud to become that Universe, this is the 15 Chakra Energy System, this is the Bodily or Physical Ascension of the Mind/Body/Spirit, or Soul Complex.

Our Spiritual Nature

So as a Soul, we are defined by our Spiritual Nature, we are Spiritual Beings inside of an Earth Created Body, we are made of the Universe, so we are it's children, and as you will learn, we go back to become that Universe, everything is Interconnected, now that we know this, we can see how what we do effects other around us, as EVE, our Thoughts are Powerful, for our ideas go on to make great things, but we are more than our Mind or our Body, we were made in the Image or imagination of the Heavenly Power, both Male and Female, so this should explain how we see the Higher Powers as Mom and Dad, when we Soul Jump from the Heavens, we are a baby, and we forget that our vital information is written on our DNA, and opened with Faith, so we walk around living vicariously, and we keep having to come back to Earth for Karmic Purposes, once these Karmic Attachments and Obligations are broken, we can then fully Ascend, but we must look on our DNA for the Answers, why is this happening to me? Ask your DNA this question, and it will bring to your mind the answer, this is the Super Conscious Mind at work, the Universal Mind we all share, and we all contribute thoughts to the Storehouse of Knowledge and Wisdom, once they have confirmed it's validity, it is accepted, and added to the information already there, this is our Collective Conscious, our Universal Intelligence, giving us the Answers to our questions or prayers, this is what Spirituality, the Science of GOD is all about, reconnecting us humans back to the Power that created us, and as we explore the dimensions of the mind, and we see how our Intelligence grows, 1 day, we will escape Dimensionality, and become 1 with the

Unified Sound Field or Yunasai, the finality of the Feminine Energy, and after that we reach the Great Beyond, the finality of the Masculine Energy, and then we become the Founders, as we continue to Infinity and Beyond.

The Spiritual Ascension

So now let's start this Multi Dimensional examination of our various Minds and the Spiritual Parts of the Ascension Process, these will describe the conditions of our Soul, and how they relate to GOD and getting us back to the Source or Power that created us, this is the Spiritual Ascension, the Mental Ascension will open up your Consciousness, Learning about the

Divine Pair will allow you to Awaken your Kundalini, then the Physical Ascension will allow you to Activate your Chakras, and as you do that, you build faith which will Unlock your Advanced DNA, you will then begin to fully open your Third Eye, which is our Higher Mental Abilities, and our Psychic Powers, once you take the Limits or Limiting beliefs out your Brain, you will see that anything is possible, and then the Emotional Ascension will get you to 100% Integrity or Purity of Soul, necessary to reach the Higher Heavens, so 1D is where we first start to realize how to work with our Sub Conscious Mind, this part of the mind is responsible for all of our automatic functions, it is like a Hard Drive in a computer, it stores all of our cellular memory, and it has constantly been recording our whole Life from Womb to Tomb, The Book of Life Recording, for our Judgment in Heaven, but you can reprogram your Sub Conscious Mind using powerful affirmation repeatedly, to change any bad habit, it usually takes about 30 to 45 days to change a long established habit, 2D is our Emotional or Instinctual Mind often called our Heart, and the center of Love, if you have Love than Faith will come, and the first 2 connect to where we are now as an incarnate soul, this is 3D Life or the 3rd Dimension, and it is where life as we know it occurs, this is called our Conscious Mind Matrix or Conscious Reality, and it is how we perceive this matrix that determines whether we will ascend after this life here on earth, or whether we will have to continually reincarnate for Karmic Purposes, but if you develop faith in this Life, it is always possible for you to ascend higher and not have to repeat a jump for Karmic Purposes, reaching your Higher Consciousness will show you or teach you how, and it is all internal or working on the Inner You, this book should have given you a start on this process, so 3D Life is our Conscious Reality, so now we go to 4D, and we start to Discover our Soul, and this is where we start to open up our Super Conscious Mind or GOD Mind, when we get here spiritually we are starting to develop our Intuition, or what is called Intuitive Knowing, where we are guided away from trouble, by the feelings in our body as they start to communicate with us thru our creative imagination, example, I am talking to a friend, and suddenly I feel a pain in my back, the conversation has taken a negative turn, and my body is telling me thru the Fight or Flight System to leave immediately, I do, and I hear later that my friend was killed because he was drunk and wouldn't calm down, if I was out there I would probably be dead too, this is how our Intuition works, 5D is called our Archetypal Mind, and it is here where we decide what type of person we will become, the Church, the Teacher, the Ruler, the Magician, the Businessman, or The Servant, you have to decide what life you are gonna live, and this is where you make this decision, each archetype has it's strengths and weakness, and most decide to explore different possibilities each time they incarnate on Earth, if you have passed away, there is still gonna be opportunities after Ascension for your Soul to go back to earth for the Purpose of the Archetypal Lessons, 6D is called the Celestial Mind, and as you start to become 1 with the Universe that made you, you will start to develop what is called Inner Vision and Increased Clarity, also called Our 3rd Eye and our Psychic Powers, here you are becoming better and so the test get harder, your Vibration is increasing and it is here where you make a decision, that will govern your future growth, it is what we call the Polarity Level, here you start to learn about Polarities, Negative (A Service to Self Mentality) and Positive (A Service to Others Mentality), each decision results in a different outcome each time we incarnate, but we never lose a lesson we previously held, it is always stored on our DNA, and opened with Faith in GOD, so this is our Soul Level Existence, if we are alive, then we are getting real close to finding out just how grand we humans are, as we leave the 6th Dimension, we arrive at the 7th, and this is where we meet the Crown, it connects directly to our GOD MIND, Our Advanced DNA, and our Crown Chakra, and this is where we find the Collective Conscious and fully connect to it, so the 7th is where we encounter what are known as the Ascended Master Teachers, and once we find our Crown, and start to realize that we are 1 with the Universe, we start to fully become part of that Universe, the Ascended Master Teachers mentally instruct us on how to develop the GOD Mind even further, and it is here where we find our Oversoul or Soul Group or Family, the people we love the most, we start to realize that we are all in this Life Thing together, The Law of One, and that realization, let's the Ascended Master Teachers know that you serious about Ascension, so they pass you on to the 8th Dimension, this is known as the Monadic Dimension, and it is where you develop your Higher Heart, you begin to Love more deeply, if we are still alive, then spiritually, we have fully left the physical body at this time, you are starting to see changes in your perception, and your psychic powers are getting stronger, and now you are getting to the Higher Dimensions, so we can think of the monad as the center point of a standing up infinity loop with 7 Lower and 7 Higher Dimensions, the Monad in the middle and we get to the number 15, so there are 7 more levels to go to escape Dimensionality and the Time and Energy Matrices, and really become 1 with GOD or the Yunasai in the Sound Matrix Level, The Unified Sound Field, the 9th Dimension is the Causal Mind, also called our Higher Mind, and this is where we start to build Up our Major Advanced DNA, it has been building all along, but now we get to our final 4 strands, and these are called our Higher Learning and Advanced Abilities, we have now fully integrated our Soul Existence, and that has led us on this spiritual path to the final level of the Over Soul, as we move higher up thru the Higher Dimensions, we are going to change into what is called Our Liquid Light Selves or Light Spiritual Body Selves (The Mer-Ka-Ba) at these next levels, we are becoming an Avatar like our Brother in Faith, Jesus Christ, an Avatar Body is simply our True Form as a Soul, the Electromagnetic Light Energy Body, or ELE, so at these next levels or dimensions, we have ascended thru 3 Density Levels in the Time Matrix, so now we come to the beginning of the Energy Matrix, the 10th Dimension is called the Christiac Mind or Christ Mind and it is here where we get our Higher Sensory Perception or HSP, this allows us to perceive Life in a whole new light, and it is also where we start to really develop our Higher Powers of Thought and Intelligence, things like Telekinesis and Levitation become easy at this Level, we are becoming like Christ in the bible, the 11th Dimension is called our Guru Mind or Buddha Mind, and it is here where we start to fully integrate into our Light Body, this is a Level of Oneness with The Ascended Master Teacher's and GOD, since we are going to be graduating soon from this dimensional existence, here you tell yourself which power you want to use, and then your mind shows you how to make it happen, this is Called the Guru Principle, and the 11th Strand of our Advanced DNA, the 12th Dimension is called the Nirvaniac Dimension, and it is here where we find a Higher Peace of Mind, we have evolved to our Highest Physical Point, either alive or deceased, and at the next level, we learn what it is all for, but before we get there, let me explain the 12th Dimension, this is the GOD Dimension, so called because we have fully opened or unlocked our 12 Strand Advanced DNA, fully integrated the Light Body Form, fully awakened our Kundalini Light Cord, and fully opened 12 of the 15 chakras and we will soon have our Full Aura or Auric Body, we have fully explored our Highest Consciousness Level, and we have awakened our Spiritual Soul and learned about all of our Higher Powers of Thought and Intelligence, we have risen thru 4 Density Levels, and there is only 3 more Dimensions, before we get back to the Sound and Higher Energy Matrix or Yunasai, when we reach the Highest Dimensions, we no longer require a Body, we are actually becoming 1 with the Universe, we call this the start of the Divine Gateway, so the 13th Dimension is called our Mother Arc or Planetary Arc, and it is the first level of our reintegration back to the GOD Source from which we came, so at the Mother Arc, the Finality of the Feminine Energy, we actually become our own Planetary Body, just like the Earth thru Transmigration, ever wonder what those stars are, that is us in our true form, this is why the Universe is still expanding, the 14th Dimension is called the Solar Arc or Sun Arc, The Finality of the Masculine Energy, where we integrate back into our Solar Selves, our Higher Self, we are becoming the Suns and Daughters of GOD literally, we now get to the 15th Dimension, the last Dimensional Level, we will ever experience, The Father Arc or Universal Arc, and it is here where we become that which we see, we actually become our Own Universe, and we are in charge of that Universe, we have fully evolved back to the Universe from whence we came, this is how Life works for all beings in the Universe, and every being has to go thru the same lessons, they are just learned in a different order, as we leave the Dimensions, we start to become Non Sentient or Omniscient, meaning we are just High Level Consciousness and

Energy, and we will become the Sound Matrix or Yunasai, in about a billion years, so these are the Dimensions of the Soul or the Spiritual Part of the Mind/Body/Spirit or Soul Complex, so these dimensions explain how our mind gets stronger as we learn each dimension, we start to learn to make better decisions on how we will live our lives, and we start to master each dimension, each time we graduate to another dimension, the test get harder, because we are becoming like the Power that made us, so we must become stronger and purer as a result, and this is how it is done, we will all become the Universe that made us, it is why we are here in the 1st place, we are the Universe.

Our Emotional Characteristics

So we are put on Earth to learn how to deal with adversity as we grow up and learn our life and spiritual lessons, we do this by gaining control of our emotional response to the things that are happening around us, we have to learn how to not overreact, every time that something unexpected happens, we must learn how to remain calm, and use both sides of our brain to handle this situation, we logically ask a question, then we creatively solve that problem, and if we are aware of our emotional responses, we are becoming a man of peace, a man with Emotional Intelligence, and this is the final piece of the Ascension puzzle, the Emotional Ascension is the main part, Because the opposite of Life is Death, and that is what we don't want, so learning this part will prepare you for when you arrive in Heaven at the end of this Life, and you are passed thru into the Light and can go to the higher parts of our Heavenly Home of the Soul, and relax for a short time as you receive additional schooling for your next Soul Jump, most of us will be forced to go back to the planet to pay our karmic obligations, remember this, Karma is undefeated and will never be cheated, it is our reward and punishment system and it does not give exceptions, everyone must pay the same price for their transgression upon another Soul, by being subjected to the same treatment you gave another, sorta like so we know how it feels to have wrong done to us, so we stop doing wrong to others, a perfect lesson for us to understand that our actions have consequences, and this is it, once we have completed this part of the Process, you will be Pure of Heart and operating at the right frequency to Achieve Ascension, as you will be operating at 100% Positive Polarity or Purity, and you will be able to be in the Presence of our Heavenly Power, so let's get this lesson started.

The Emotional Ascension

So this is the final part of the Ascension Process, The Emotional or Sacral Ascension, Understanding Ascension is the Key to actually Ascending, so I wrote this part called The Road to Ascension, the final piece of the puzzle and it Starts by First Believing in the Power and Light of GOD, or what we call the Yunasai, what we have called The Universal or Infinite Intelligence, this is an Intelligent Universe, some chaos, but still in order for a GOD like ours, Our GOD is Great, Our God is only Good, and the more we learn on earth, about the GOD that which is in our Hearts, the closer we get to GOD in Heaven, I bring up the name Jesus Christ, because I want you to identify what I am doing as similar, but not directly like the Father or Messiah of Earthly Religions, True Spirituality is a Science that explains religious text and concepts, in a truthful and loving way, because the Science of Faith is Universal Love, the same love we get from the Heavens, is the same love, we should give to others, and this is how we Ascend, we learn the Universal, Natural, and Spiritual Laws of the Universe, for which the Law of Attraction fame is from and Karma, often called Cause and Effect, these are 2 different Laws, but closely related to one another, but Karma is the Soul, and Cause and Effect is our actions and the consequences we face, these Universal Laws couldn't be silenced, and were going to eventually be discovered, but the evil ones, hid this information for centuries, These Universal Laws guide you on how to live a right life like Jesus Christ did in the biblical record in today's society, by separating your religious beliefs, from your scientific beliefs, and asking yourself, is this the right information?, you will have your answer, how do I know this information, well my own information and knowledge comes to me from my God Mind or Super Conscious Field, that is attached to my Advanced DNA, that is only unlocked with Faith in GOD completely, letting go of earthly attitudes, and adopting a more mature emotionally intelligent man, who fears nothing, and easily handles any challenge, living like this is called Positive Polarity, but let me give you the story, it all starts with Hope or Hopefulness, Believing that GOD is there for you, and GOD is in your Heart, so you are 1 with GOD, This Hope leads to Calm Optimism, which gives you Curiosity to find out who you are, it is written on your DNA, and only opened with Faith, this gives you Peace, which makes Life Serene, and you are pleased with yourself, and the Lord, so now your daily talks with the Lord become

Playful, your best friend, and they are always
Positive talks with GOD, this Faith helps you to
Organize your Life, and it gives you the
Courage to keep trying, once you gain
Acceptance of the things you can't change, you
don't get angry, you just build a stronger Belief
in GOD, by doing this you become more
Productive, and you even have Expectations, of
more good you can do with more money, this
drives you to Success, once there you see
Happiness, and you feel real Security, as GOD
protects us, you are starting to feel Worthy of
riches and wealth, not just in the form of money,
your Life becomes Cheerful, you now know that
you can open your DNA, so now you are
constantly Learning about new things, and
gaining Self Love, which starts to build your
Enthusiasm, which leads you to feel Good, and
so you now have Gratitude to the Lord for all
that the power has given you, this appreciation
to the Lord leads to the Lord doing more for you

which brings you Confidence, you learn you can do anything with Positive Self Talk, even though you have Power and Success now, you still try to operate with Humility, you still wanna help others, when you do this, they say you Seek For Good, and then you start seeing Good in everybody and everything, you are now becoming Powerful, and your Soul is alive, you feel Joy for the first time, or laughter on the inside of you near the stomach, at this point your Success is coming, so GOD says to you, let's be and learn some Patience, I can move Mountains for you, but thru natural processes, all things take time, you wait a short time for Success to come, and when it comes, it brings you Freedom from worry, no more suffering, this is called Mercy and Grace, and now you have Full Trust in the Lord, you are ready to work with the Lord to turn people to the Light of GOD, and away from the darkness, now as you get Wealth, you start to become Generous, helping others with your money, so more builds due to Natural Law, and now your Love for Humanity is Outward Focused, to the whole entire Cosmos or Universe, other Souls in Heaven start to take notice of this human, they are Amazed, they seen this type of commitment a few times in Heaven in that name Jesus Christ and some others, he is almost home, but he is still alive and enjoying Life, this is wonderful, he can teach us some Life Lessons, he got on his Earthly Journey, this is where you unlock your Advanced DNA, it is how I write these books in less than a week, and you gain all of this additional Knowledge, and you start to be of Positive Polarity or Service to Others Mentality, this is how the Christ lived in service to others, at this point, your love of GOD becomes A Passion, The Passion of the Christ, and with the Lord inside you, you feel Empowerment, all you focus on is Abundance, and now you know intuitively that you are the Victor, and this is the

Ultimate Victory, to get back to our Parents in Heaven, GOD, when you see others suffer now, you start to feel Empathy and want to help the less fortunate, you tell them to forgive others, and GOD will forgive them, this is the only way, this is due to Natural Law, at this point in your Spiritual journey, you have learned Compassion for others less fortunate, one of the bigger lessons is too love others, even the most vile evil ratchet demon needs some semblance of Love, All things come From God, All types and species of human like come from GOD, and they all have Free Will, it is a Universal Law, a Natural Law, this has to happen, for that to happen type Law, at this Point you have Ascended to the Highest Level a Human can reach in this Lifetime, and because your Light is on, you are Radiant, and Full of GOD, for GOD is the Light, you now fully accept the Universal Love for All Icon app, remember this, turn it on like a smartphone simply by saying and believing these words to your self, this is called true Faith "I Love The Universe, My Family, Like I Love Myself", if the Universe is Family, you will protect your Family, this is the LOGOS of the entire COSMOS or Multiple Universes, however you write it, at this point, you have achieved Mental and Emotional Ascension to your Liquid Light Energy Form at 100% Integrity, Total Positive Polarity, what we call Purity for GOD is Pure Love, Energy, Intelligence, and Power, so the only way to be in the Presence of this Love and Light is to be Pure of Heart, now you have traveled Beyond the 15th Dimension, where you sit with Jesus Christ, by the Side of your Parents or GOD Till Infinity, the entire Universe or Cosmos is a never ending Story, this was demonstrated in the biblical record by Jesus Christ after his death and resurrection, and The Soul of man will rise to the Heavens, The Image below will show you the Polarity Chart I mentioned.

EMOTIONAL SPIRAL
ASCENDING

Unconditional-Love	100% Integrity
Empathy Forgiveness	Compassion Radiant
Passion Empowerment	Abundance Victor
Generous Outward-Focused	Knowledge Service
Powerful Joy Patient	Freedom Trust
Confidence Positive-Self-Talk	Humility Seek-for-Good
Learning Self-love	Enthusiasm Gratitude
Happiness Security	Worthy Cheerful
Acceptance Belief	Productive Expectation
Playful Positive	Organize Courage
Curiosity Peace	Serene Pleased
Hopefulness	Calm Optimism
Boredom	Boredom
Overwhelm Fear	Jealousy Frustration
Insecurity Pessimism	Judgment Self-pity
Grief Unsupported	Revenge Anger
Failure Hatred	Doubt Depression
Heartache Rejection	Impatience Worry
Depression Disappointment	Negative-Self-Talk
Despair Discouragement	Blame Sorrow
Worthless Humiliation	Irritation Helplessness
Low-Self-Esteem Victim	Bitterness Dread
Unworthiness Shame	Guilt Apathy
No-Will-to-Live	Death

DESCENDING

What Comes after Ascension

So Ascension is the Key to getting back to the side of our Heavenly Parents or GOD, and truly being able to understand just why we were put on Earth, all of these lessons will make us a most caring Power, when it is our turn to lead a Universe, we are created from a piece of ELI, the Huge Ball of Lightning that started this never ending story of our Universe, and we will become just like ELI over many billions of years, so we all will once again reform the whole and we will all finally get to an Infinity Level Existence, the true definition of Heaven, once total Positive Polarity is learned by all of the Earth's citizens, so it is up to the 1's of us who are enlightened on these subjects to teach others about our greatness, and wake everybody up to these new possibilities, and that is what this book is for, to show you a new way to build your Mind, a new way to communicate with this higher presence, a new way to see Life and all the beauty of this Universe, we will one day become, this is fabulous news for those who have never heard this, many people ask me how did I figure out ELI was the creator in my last book, and I told them that as Jesus Christ laid upon the cross, and took his final breath, "he said ELI, ELI, why has thou forsaken me", but ELI had not forsaken the Christ, it was time for his ELE to exit the Body, and this was the transition period, so our Savior and brother died and now we can piece together the rest of the story that is to be found in the book.

The Summary of Master Everything

So as we have read in this book, we can learn how to master everything, if we just use the Super Conscious Mind to come up with the Idea, and use the Sub Conscious Mind to make it automatic, we will have mastered that power, this is how we build our psychic powers, by using Higher Learning and the Guru Principle and reading books that connect us emotionally, we feel like the author is telling the truth, and so we take it into the Sub Conscious, and it becomes a habit, it happens automatically, and now we have mastered a power, we can Unlock our DNA only with Faith in GOD, there is no other way for which I know, and when we do we can access all of the Vital Information that is locked on 10 of those 12 Strands, we also learned about our Advanced Abilities and Higher Powers of Perception, where we can see into the future, and use this knowledge to make a better decision on how we will approach a situation, we have also learned about our

Sensory Perceptions, Extra Sensory Perception, our 6th sense, and Higher Sensory Perception, our 7th Sense, and we learned what they are, and we also have learned the Secrets or Pillars of Ascension, it is what Jesus Christ is said to have went thru in the bible, and it is real, all of this information is of the highest regards, and as we come to the close of this book, I just want you to know that you can really Master Everything, when you learn to use the Power of Your Mind, and once you learn that, you will know that our Thoughts Become Things, so now we can live in a positive world, and that will become our reality, when we walk out our door, I would like to thank everybody who reads this, and I would like to send everybody a Thank you for your purchase of this great book, we are all 1, Thanks for reading this.

The Book Case and Bookstore

My Name is David Solomon Brown, but I also use the name David DaVinci, this sets me apart from other writers with the same name, and when I look back on my life, I realized that I had a lot of good memories, I was always successful, at being the leader of some group of my friends, that is who I am, always been confident, but that was when I realized that confidence wasn't my problem, I always loved God, so Faith wasn't my problem, so what was wrong, it was all of those Limiting Beliefs, that I carried around with me, from the womb, old repressed memories, and old stories I remember, that might not be true anymore, if my teacher, said I wasn't smart, I would show her my straight A report card, then tell my mom to beat her up, my Mom was too sweet a person, and only knew how to help people, so I am following in her footsteps, the sad thing is most people carry it around, all the pain and trauma is real, but you still have to let it go, that is what is causing your disease and sickness, all pain in the body, apart from injuries you suffered in an accident is negative thoughts, anger, and negative emotions, and you carry it around with you as emotional baggage, you can't put it down, forgive them like God forgives you, then move on with the good life God has planned for you, you stay in the cycle, womb to tomb, lifetime after lifetime facing the same problems over and over, but all you had to do, was ask GOD personally and in private, to show you the way, then learn how to listen to your heart, your mind, your body, they all give signs, that tell you something is wrong with the computer, it has a virus, and we need the anti virus software, that is written in the Guidebook "For Those Who Were Poor, But

Dream For More", the Universal or Natural Laws are real, and awareness of them is crucial to knowing the rules of this new reality, and cycle we are now in, remember that they can not be changed, this is how the Universe works, how do I know, I study the Universe, I wrote a book that details, 52 of them called "The Big Book of Universal Laws" that gives you all of the information, to live your life right, the next book is called 'I 1 or (I Won)", it is a Mindset Book, that's put you in the Right Mindset, for success to come to you easily, after that I wrote, "The Answer, The Book Of ELI", in that book, I told the story of our early start from just before the Big Bang, I also talked about Universal Love, Soul Growth, and the Law of One, explained in the book of laws, now in the Guidebook, I talk about an astral projection dream that led me to my understanding of the Heavenly Power, that information was what I was trying to communicate in that book, the next book was about our minds, our goals, our powers of perception, or Third Eye Activation, that book is called "The Power of your Thoughts", the next book is called "The Truth about Everything", and this book was designed by me to give you the real Truth about Everything. It gave you real facts and stories that not even the highest thinkers on the planet can remember, and it is filled with a lot of truth, the next book was called the "The Science of Spirituality", and it told you what Spirituality is, and how to really figure out who you are, the next book was called "A Spiritual Understanding, The True GOD Code Explained" in it I gave you, real subjects like the truth about Creation and the Origins of Evil, my next book was called "The Key of David, The True DNA Code", and talked to people about turning your so called Junk DNA into an Advanced DNA, and how this system works, I have also written as part of my Legacy Series of books, my 1st Novel called Wealth,

Women, and Weapons In the L.I.F.E. Living In Financial Excellence, which talks about my Fascinating Life and My Musical Career, and my new book called "Understanding The Collective Conscious, Exploring the Storehouse of Knowledge and Wisdom in Heaven", which will show you how to communicate with our Collective Conscious, called the Universal or Infinite Intelligence, all the answers you seek are in the Storehouse, and this book will give you some Knowledge, Wisdom, and Understanding about Spirituality, the next book was called "Secrets of the Super Conscious Mind, and the Key to unlocking the GOD Mind", and the Advanced DNA that it is attached to, the next book was called "Breaking Karma – Reincarnation Explained" and talked about how we go from Reincarnation to Ascension as we break our Karmic Obligations and Attachments, after that I wrote "Universal Creation and The Reason for Existence", in it I explain the entire process from just before the big bang to the present, the How and Why we were created, my next book was called "The Law of 1 and a New Hope for Humanity", in it I told you about this Universal Law, and how by living in this way, we could overcome many of the problems facing society, after that I wrote "As Below, So Above- The War in the Heavens, a switch on the saying from the emerald tablets, As Above, So Below, this was so I could talk about what we do on Earth, and how it effects the Universe due to our Interconnection, my next book was called "A Journey to The Great Beyond" All the Mysteries Revealed, and it told you what GOD really is, and how the Universe was created, they say I am not a scientist or a doctor, and I laugh, and people may laugh at some of this, but I am aware that every word I say is the TRUTH, according and only to my Belief System, you can take the parts that sound right, and build your own opinion about the material in any of my books, but if there is 1 thing about me I respect, it is that I always do my research, I go above and beyond to bring you real facts, and then I can direct you to more things to help you, but you are also helping me, by purchasing my books at Kobo Plus/Human Evolution, Elevation, and Ascension, and the Self Improvement Series. Gumroad.com/richyoungfly, and at Amazon.com, in both hardback and softback and an e-book on amazon/kindle, by searching for Human Evolution, Elevation, and Ascension, The Self Improvement Series, or the Legacy Series and scrolling down, and also by writing your own, in Heaven, these books are called LESSONS, and I will continue to write books about stuff that you may of never seen or heard before, this is "Master Everything – The Power of Your Mind – How our Thoughts become Things", thanks for reading, all these books let me know that I was on the right track, and what

I was teaching to others was really valid, I'm not a doctor, but I am able to see things from a whole different perspective than most, and I just want to try and uplift others with these stories of success. So check out my other books on these sites, and to everybody, We are 1, I Love You all. To ELI, My Universal Family, My Universal Intelligence, and the Founders in the Great Beyond and the Higher Yunasai, Thanks.

Printed in Great Britain
by Amazon